Beautifully Piano

INSTRUMENTALS

ISBN 978-1-4950-3524-1

HAL•LEONARD®
CORPORATION
7777 W. BLUEMOUND RD. P.O. BOX 13819 MILWAUKEE, WI 53213

Visit Hal Leonard Online at
www.halleonard.com

YOUR FAVORITE MUSIC
ARRANGED FOR PIANO SOLO

ADELE FOR PIANO SOLO – 2ND EDITION
This collection features 13 Adele favorites beautifully arranged for piano solo, including: Chasing Pavements • Hello • Rolling in the Deep • Set Fire to the Rain • Someone like You • Turning Tables • When We Were Young • and more.
00307585 ....$14.99

PRIDE & PREJUDICE
12 piano pieces from the 2006 Oscar-nominated film, including: Another Dance • Darcy's Letter • Georgiana • Leaving Netherfield • Liz on Top of the World • Meryton Townhall • The Secret Life of Daydreams • Stars and Butterflies • and more.
00313327 ....$17.99

BATTLESTAR GALACTICA
by Bear McCreary
For this special collection, McCreary himself has translated the acclaimed orchestral score into fantastic solo piano arrangements at the intermediate to advanced level. Includes 19 selections in all, and as a bonus, simplified versions of "Roslin and Adama" and "Wander My Friends." Contains a note from McCreary, as well as a biography.
00313530 ....$17.99

GEORGE GERSHWIN – RHAPSODY IN BLUE (ORIGINAL)
Alfred Publishing Co.
George Gershwin's own piano solo arrangement of his classic contemporary masterpiece for piano and orchestra. This masterful measure-for-measure two-hand adaptation of the complete modern concerto for piano and orchestra incorporates all orchestral parts and piano passages into two staves while retaining the clarity, sonority, and brilliance of the original.
00321589 ....$16.99

THE BEST JAZZ PIANO SOLOS EVER
Over 300 pages of beautiful classic jazz piano solos featuring standards in any jazz artist's repertoire. Includes: Afternoon in Paris • Giant Steps • Moonlight in Vermont • Moten Swing • A Night in Tunisia • Night Train • On Green Dolphin Street • Song for My Father • West Coast Blues • Yardbird Suite • and more.
00312079 ....$19.99

ROMANTIC FILM MUSIC
40 piano solo arrangements of beloved songs from the silver screen, including: Anyone at All • Come What May • Glory of Love • I See the Light • I Will Always Love You • Iris • It Had to Be You • Nobody Does It Better • She • Take My Breath Away (Love Theme) • A Thousand Years • Up Where We Belong • When You Love Someone • The Wind Beneath My Wings • and many more.
00122112 ....$17.99

CLASSICS WITH A TOUCH OF JAZZ
Arranged by Lee Evans
27 classical masterpieces arranged in a unique and accessible jazz style. Mr Evans also provides an audio recording of each piece. Titles include: Air from Suite No. 3 (Bach) • Barcarolle "June" (Tchaikovsky) • Pavane (Faure) • Piano Sonata No. 8 "Pathetique" (Beethoven) • Reverie (Debussy) • The Swan (Saint-Saens) • and more.
00151662 Book/Online Audio $14.99

STAR WARS: THE FORCE AWAKENS
Music from the soundtrack to the seventh installment of the Star Wars® franchise by John Williams is presented in this songbook, complete with artwork from the film throughout the whole book, including eight pages in full color! Titles include: The Scavenger • Rey Meets BB-8 • Rey's Theme • That Girl with the Staff • Finn's Confession • The Starkiller • March of the Resistance • Torn Apart • and more.
00154451 ....$17.99

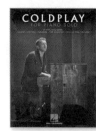

COLDPLAY FOR PIANO SOLO
Stellar solo arrangements of a dozen smash hits from Coldplay: Clocks • Fix You • In My Place • Lost! • Paradise • The Scientist • Speed of Sound • Trouble • Up in Flames • Viva La Vida • What If • Yellow.
00307637 ....$15.99

TAYLOR SWIFT FOR PIANO SOLO – 2ND EDITION
This updated second edition features 15 of Taylor's biggest hits from her self-titled first album all the way through her pop breakthrough album, *1989*. Includes: Back to December • Blank Space • Fifteen • I Knew You Were Trouble • Love Story • Mean • Mine • Picture to Burn • Shake It Off • Teardrops on My Guitar • 22 • We Are Never Ever Getting Back Together • White Horse • Wildest Dreams • You Belong with Me.
00307375 ....$16.99

DISNEY SONGS
12 Disney favorites in beautiful piano solo arrangements, including: Bella Notte (This Is the Night) • Can I Have This Dance • Feed the Birds • He's a Tramp • I'm Late • The Medallion Calls • Once Upon a Dream • A Spoonful of Sugar • That's How You Know • We're All in This Together • You Are the Music in Me • You'll Be in My Heart (Pop Version).
00313527 ....$14.99

UP
Music by Michael Giacchino
Piano solo arrangements of 13 pieces from Pixar's mammoth animated hit: Carl Goes Up • It's Just a House • Kevin Beak'n • Married Life • Memories Can Weigh You Down • The Nickel Tour • Paradise Found • The Small Mailman Returns • The Spirit of Adventure • Stuff We Did • We're in the Club Now • and more, plus a special section of full-color artwork from the film!
00313471 ....$17.99

GREAT THEMES FOR PIANO SOLO
Nearly 30 rich arrangements of popular themes from movies and TV shows, including: Bella's Lullaby • Chariots of Fire • Cinema Paradiso • The Godfather (Love Theme) • Hawaii Five-O Theme • Theme from "Jaws" • Theme from "Jurassic Park" • Linus and Lucy • The Pink Panther • Twilight Zone Main Title • and more.
00312102 ....$14.99

Prices, content, and availability subject to change without notice.
Disney Characters and Artwork TM & © 2018 Disney

HAL•LEONARD®
7777 W. Bluemound Rd. P.O. Box 13819 Milwaukee, WI 53213
www.halleonard.com

CONTENTS

PIANO SOLO

BACK TO LIFE

By GIOVANNI ALLEVI

Moderato ♩ = c. 88

mp

With pedal

mf

BEYOND

By WILLIAM JOSEPH
and DAVID FOSTER

CHARIOTS OF FIRE
from CHARIOTS OF FIRE

By VANGELIS

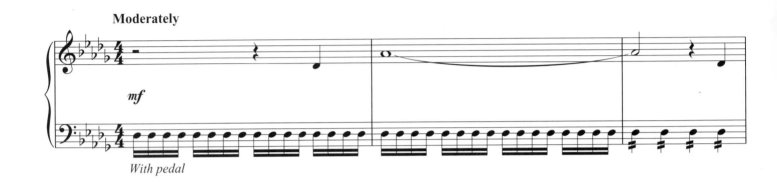

COURAGE OF THE WIND

By DAVID LANZ

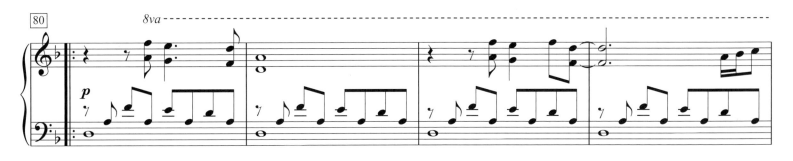

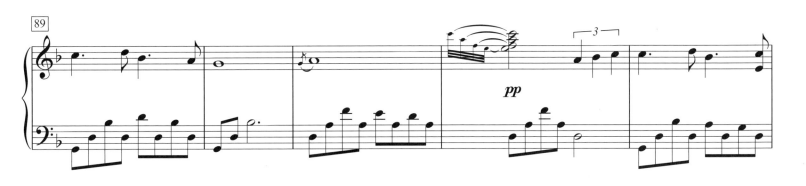

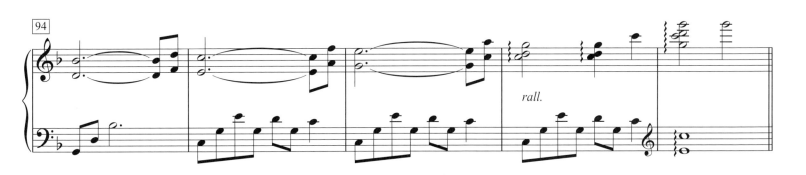

THE HEART ASKS PLEASURE FIRST

from THE PIANO

By MICHAEL NYMAN

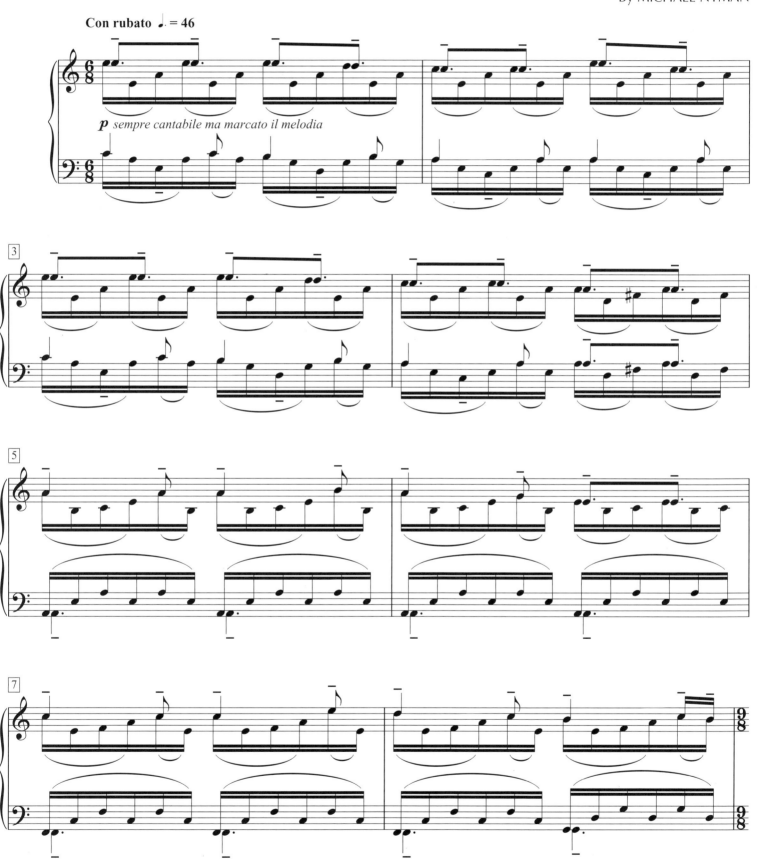

24

26

p sempre marcato il melodia

CROSSROADS

By JIM BRICKMAN

A DAY WITHOUT RAIN

By ENYA
and NICKY RYAN

I GIORNI

By LUDOVICO EINAUDI

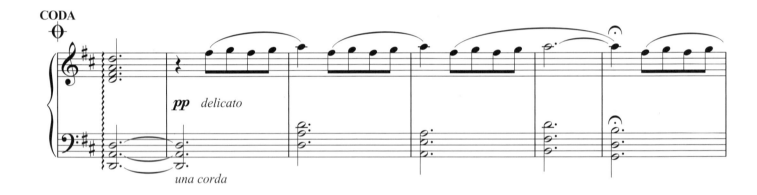

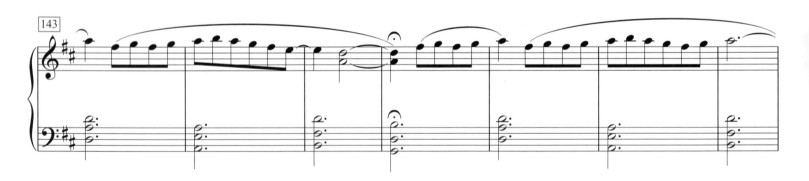

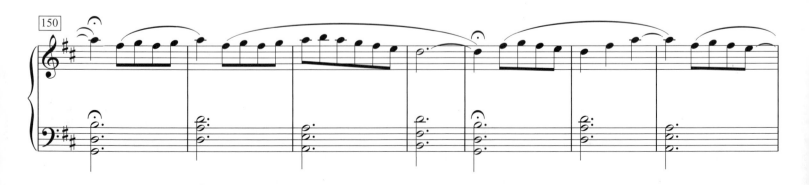

IF YOU BELIEVE

Composed by
JIM BRICKMAN

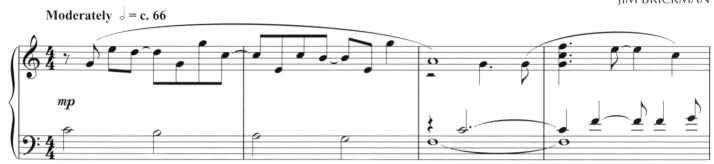

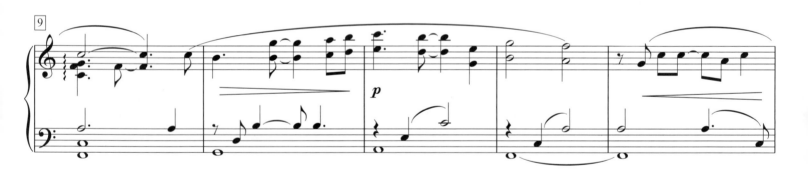

45

LA VALSE D'AMELIE

from AMELIE

By YANN TIERSEN

LEAVES ON THE SEINE

By DAVID LANZ

52

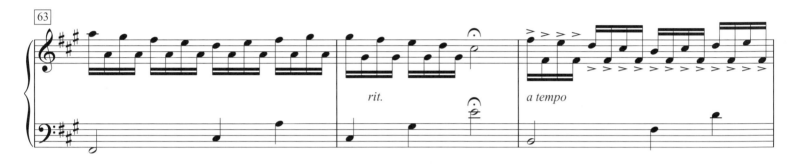

LOVE ME

By YIRUMA

MORNING PASSAGES
from THE HOURS

By PHILIP GLASS

60

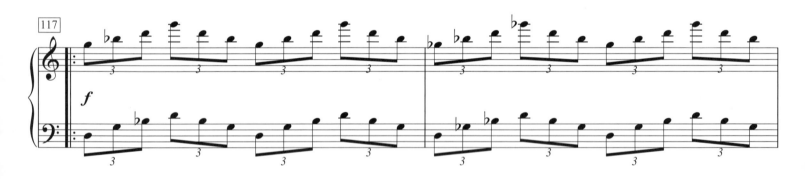

MUSIC BOX DANCER

Composed by FRANK MILLS

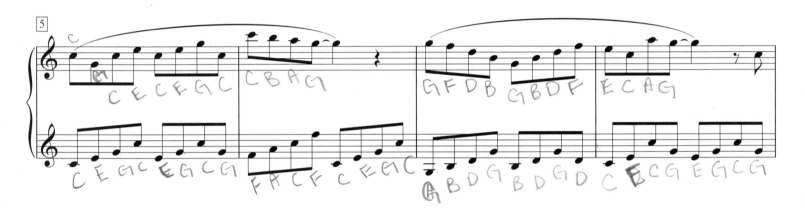

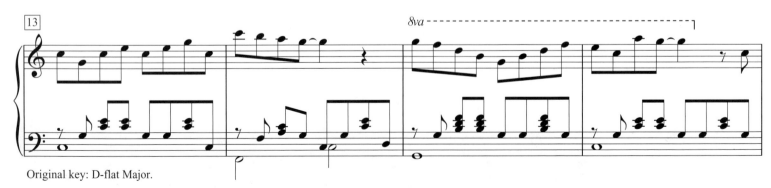

Original key: D-flat Major.

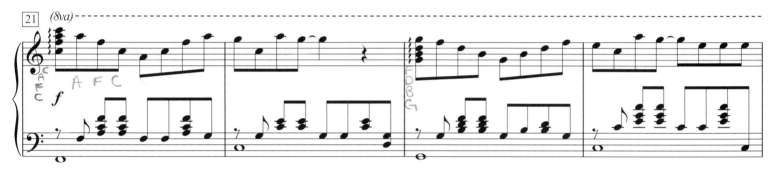

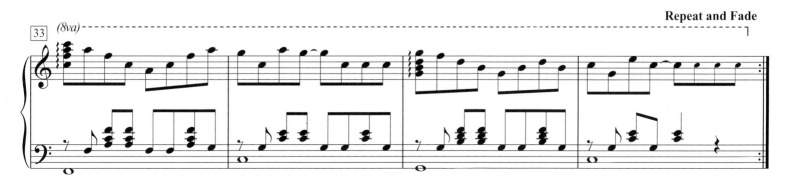

NUVOLE BIANCHE

Music by LUDOVICO EINAUDI

70

THE PARK ON PIANO
from FINDING NEVERLAND

By JAN KACZMAREK

ONE MAN'S DREAM

Composed by
YANNI

Evenly, with an inward intensity ♩ = 120

RETURN TO THE HEART

By DAVID LANZ

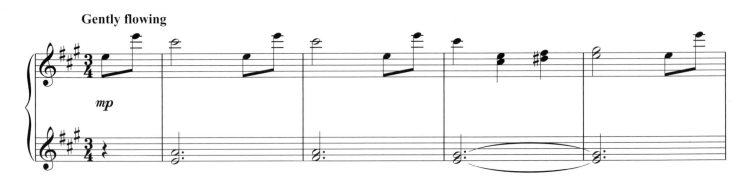

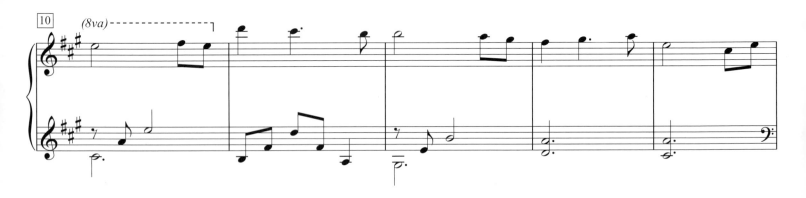

RIVER FLOWS IN YOU

By YIRUMA

Freely, flowing

Moderately, expressively

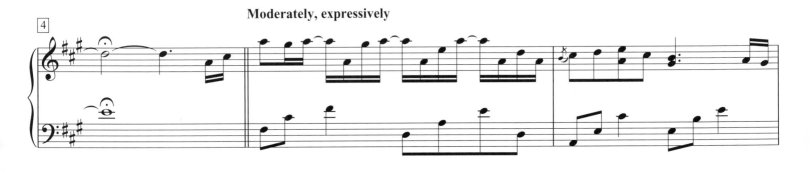

SUCH GOOD LUCK
from the Television Series DOWNTON ABBEY

By JOHN LUNN

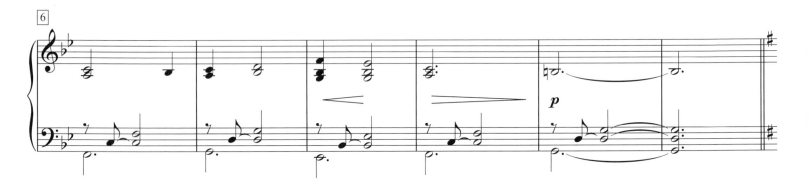

SUR LE FIL
from AMELIE

By YANN TIERSEN

Rubato ♩ = c. 92

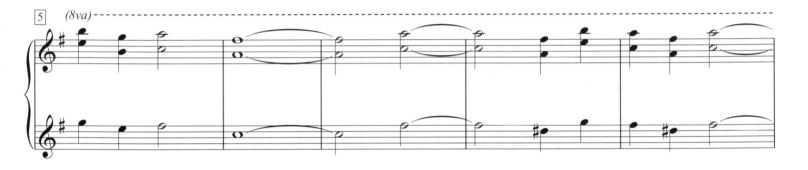

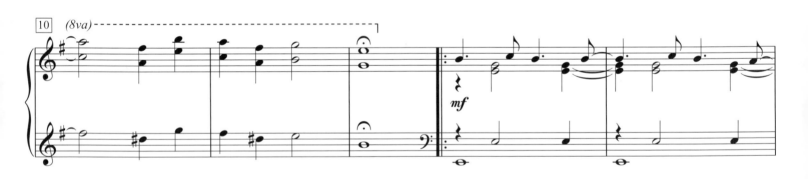

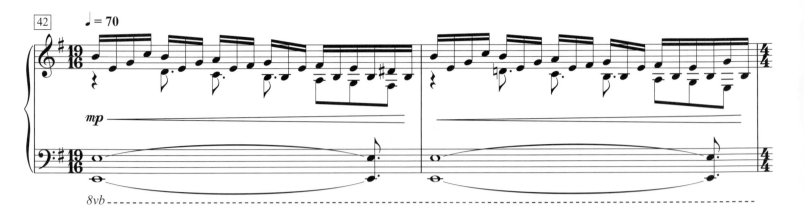

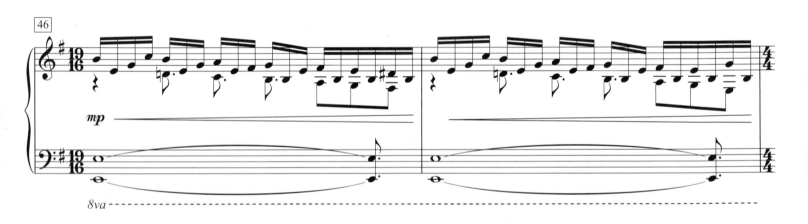

93

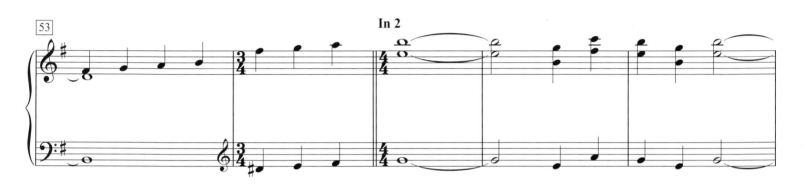

TOGETHER WE WILL LIVE FOREVER
from THE FOUNTAIN

By CLINT MANSELL

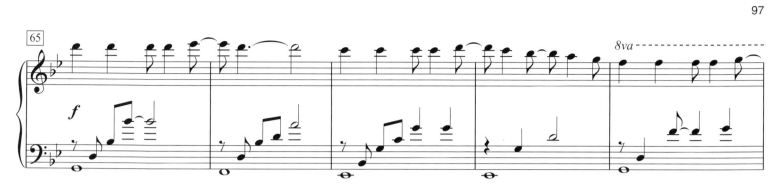

WITH MALICE TOWARD NONE

from the Motion Picture LINCOLN

Composed by JOHN WILLIAMS

With simple expression

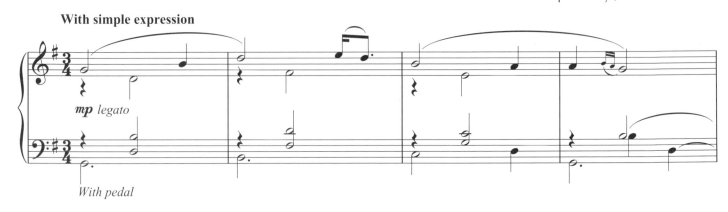

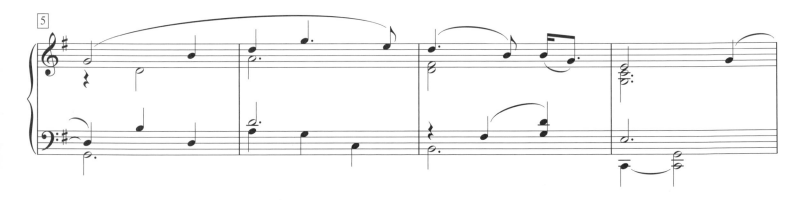

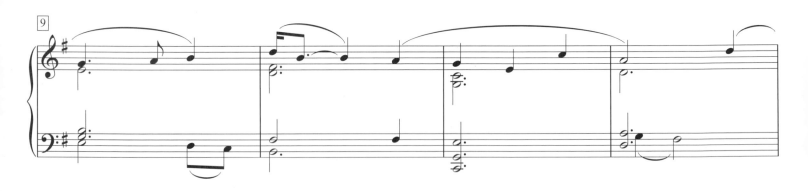

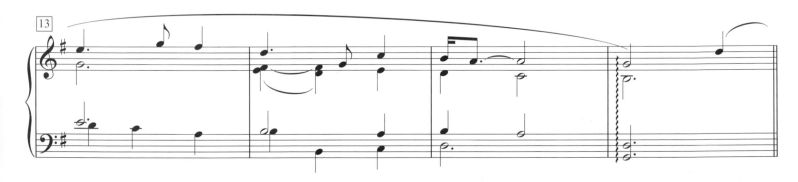

ZANARKAND

By NOBUO UEMATSU

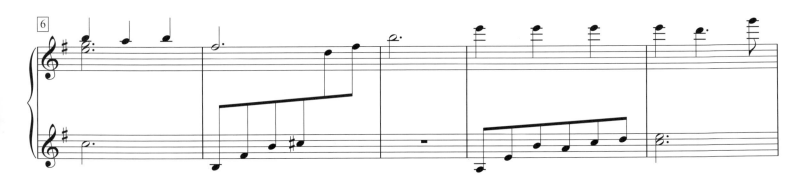

PIANO *and* CELLO

As performed by The Piano Guys

ARWEN'S VIGIL

By JON SCHMIDT,
STEVEN SHARP NELSON
and AL VAN DER BEEK

(No pedal lift here.)